GAZOZ

The Art of Making Magical,
Seasonal Sparkling Drinks

GAZOZ

BENNY BRIGA &
ADEENA SUSSMAN

Photography by Dan Perez
Illustrations by David Schiller

ARTISAN BOOKS
New York

Library of Congress Cataloging-in-Publication Data
is on file.

ISBN 978-1-57965-875-5

Cover and text design by Toni Tajima
Cover photographs by Dan Perez

Artisan books are available at special discounts
when purchased in bulk for premiums and sales
promotions as well as for fund-raising or educational
use. Special editions or book excerpts also can be
created to specification. For details, contact the
Special Sales Director at the address below, or send
an e-mail to specialmarkets@workman.com.

For speaking engagements,
contact speakersbureau@workman.com.

Published by Artisan
A division of Workman Publishing Co., Inc.
225 Varick Street
New York, NY 10014-4381
artisanbooks.com

Artisan is a registered trademark of
Workman Publishing Co., Inc.

Published simultaneously in Canada by
Thomas Allen & Son, Limited

Printed in China

First printing, April 2021

1 3 5 7 9 10 8 6 4 2

CONTENTS

INTRODUCTION

Gazoz
ga·zoz | \gə'zóz\
a carbonated nonalcoholic drink

OUT OF MY TINY, postage stamp–size shop in Tel Aviv, surrounded by an ever-growing apothecary derived from nature's bounty, I have developed a cultish culture around the fizzy power of bubbles. Every day, hundreds of people from all over the world approach the counter and order a glass of gazoz: a gorgeous, aromatic, colorful, zero-proof, and altogether tantalizing beverage of fruit, fizz, flora, and fermentation—liquid magic whose name is derived from the Turkish word for "gas."

Seltzer, soda water, bubbly water—whatever you call it—is having a moment. In the past few years seltzer has become incredibly popular, and (in my very biased opinion) for very good reason. Lacking the artificial coloring and flavoring of conventional sodas and other beverages, clear, crisp seltzer and seltzer-based drinks are lighter, healthier, and more balanced than their conventional alternatives. Refreshing, caffeine-free, nonalcoholic, and fun, these seltzer-based drinks are something anyone of any age can enjoy at any time of day.

The gazoz drinks that I make in my shop—and that I am sharing with you here—let you ride this current wave of seltzer love. By combining seltzer, ice, fruit, homemade syrups, fermentations, and other flavorings in a tall glass, you can elevate that glass of fizz into a custom creation that speaks to your individual tastes and allows you to flex your creative muscles.

With gazoz you can always customize—picking the fruit, level of sweetness, and variety of flavors—to get the drink you want to have at the moment you want to drink it. And you will want to drink gazoz *all the time*. Especially when it's hot … but not *only* then. We're all trying to increase the amount of water we drink each day, and a glass of gazoz gets you there. Kids want a soda? Give them a colorful,

1

flavor-filled gazoz instead. Looking for a five-o'clock-somewhere treat but not interested in a buzz? The answer is gazoz.

Nature Is My Muse

First and foremost, these beverages are intended to slake your thirst, but making one has the added effect of jump-starting the imagination of whoever is making the creation.

I am blessed to see inspiration for gazoz everywhere I turn, but it's the intersection of the urban and the wild that inspires me the

most. Many of us, including myself, live in cities. But rather than be cut off from nature, if we merely open our eyes to breathe, smell, touch, absorb, and observe, there is beauty to be found in plain sight: flowers, herbs, and fruit can all be picked and added to a glass of gazoz.

The fresh fruits and vegetables, spices, leaves, and flowers that are at the heart of my creations are the essence of life, something you can celebrate at home by making your very own glasses of gazoz. Where I live, beautiful produce is available year-round. But it is not a requirement, and that's the beauty of gazoz. Whether you have something as simple as a berry or as sophisticated as a dragon fruit, the resulting drink will be delicious. Whether you're foraging in a forest or coasting with your cart in a supermarket produce aisle, you'll find what you need to make the perfect sparkling drink.

Sweet Fermentation

I call the process of suspending fruit in sugar, then watching it take new form over time, sweet fermentation. Fermenting is a process of deprivation and its happy results, when the absence of oxygen and the presence of sugar and the natural yeasts that live in our environment combine in the jar to produce fruit that concentrates in its own flavor, then deepens as fermentation ensues. The complexity of the process, and the equally complex results, lends counterbalance and layered flavor to my glasses of gazoz—and are delicious (and healthy) enjoyed on their own.

Sweet fermentation is about capturing the beauty of nature. A glass of gazoz is the process of nature, arrested and captured in a glass. No two glasses are the same, even if they contain the same ingredients, since the force of nature causes molecular changes even from second to second.

Nature in Motion

Every drink I make is crafted in the moment, but in truth it contains weeks, months, and sometimes years of maceration, fermentation, and resting time—slowly developed flavor that comes together perfectly in every glass.

In addition to fermented and fresh fruits, my gazoz drinks contain aromatic herbs and leaves procured from the market, foraged in fields, or raised in our own tiny organic garden in Tel Aviv. The sparkling drinks often contain a splash of kombucha, kefir, and jun, of-the-moment fermented beverages I've been making for years (see page 59). These elements can change depending on the season and your whims, but one thing is certain: There will be bubbles. Life-affirming, tongue-tickling bubbles of seltzer, tiny globes of carbon dioxide floating to the surface, adding a microdose of effervescent life to every sip.

Ever since I was a child, I've been drawn to flowers, plants, fruits, and herbs, their beauty and unpredictability my ultimate comfort zone. I grew up not far from Tel Aviv, in a blue-collar town that had a low-tech magic all its own. There was one street, one bus line, one bank, no supermarket, and dozens of ethnic restaurants serving honest, delicious food.

My Turkish Israeli mother made her own heady, perfumed rose jam from blooms she foraged from the neighborhood, when children still roamed free in the fragrant fields all around, and before highways and housing projects created long shadows from the hot summer sun. On the way home from school, my friends and I would follow the gentle bend of the local river, which swelled during the rainy season. We ran between carob trees oozing syrup from their trunks and would collect butterflies in our palms as we sought out sweet lemons and blood oranges to bring home to our mothers.

On camping trips with our scout troop, we would pluck furry loquats straight from their flowering trees and eat them out of hand, the juice running down our cheeks. The sensory memories of fragrant blooms and sweet fruit were imprinted on me permanently, and it is these simple references that have informed my approach to life and work ever since, nourishing me in a multitude of ways. I see my role not as a manipulator or controller of nature, but rather as an individual privileged to harness it for the pleasure of others.

So how did my little shop and its culture of gazoz come about?

After completing my military service in Israel and traveling around the world for more than a year, I settled down in Tel Aviv, the city where I've now made my home for the past twenty years. I worked in the kitchens of some of the city's best restaurants, honing my palate and learning how to coax maximum flavor from a multitude of ingredients. At the same time I was picking wild fresh herbs whose aroma would alert me to their presence before I even saw them. Every winter I would pluck bitter oranges from communal trees dotted all over the city and sink them into sugar, preserving their beauty so I could enjoy their taste for months to come.

Eventually I opened my own restaurant, where, in addition to serving food, I infused dozens of jars of alcohol with fresh fruit to create spirits I would serve my customers at the end of a meal. I like cooking, but I *loved* preserving that fruit, watching it take on a life of its own and change a little bit every day. Those jars became my children, and after closing my restaurant, I made sure to distribute

6

them to friends and family so they could enjoy them and watch the process continue.

With the restaurant closed, I took some time to think about what I wanted to do with my life, something that would allow me to pursue my love of food while immersing myself in the world of plants, flowers, and fruits. The idea of a small shop, walking distance from my home, took hold, and I moved quickly. I chose Florentin, a gently worn neighborhood in south Tel Aviv, where I already lived. I rented a tiny space in the heart of Levinsky Street, which has a storied market of the same name and on which vendors of spices, dried fruits, and other dry goods have plied their trade since the 1930s. The neighborhood had the ideal Tel Avivian balance of old and new, tradition and progress, that made it an ideal location for what I had in mind, and for my decidedly old soul.

The market and culture that sprung up around Levinsky Street had turned it into a destination for people from all over the world, and I wanted to be a part of that excitement. I would buy as much as I could from the shopkeepers around me, taking inspiration from the neighborhood's rich history while supplying coffee and drinks to a varied community: the shopkeepers themselves, the octogenarians who had lived in Florentin for decades, and the wave of artists, musicians, and young people who had begun to make the neighborhood their home.

One of the first investments I made was the giant tank of CO_2 I had installed underneath the counter; it took up a full quarter of my storage space and could make a few thousand glasses of seltzer before it needed to be replaced. This machine got my head turning about the possibility of using that seltzer for something far more interesting than an espresso chaser.

I decorated my 6-foot-long (2 m) countertop with bins of orchids, geranium leaves, basil sprigs, and roses I'd picked myself or that people would bring me. I became easily recognizable as the crazy guy on the vintage bike, my curly hair flowing behind me, greens peeking out of my backpack and bike basket. People wondered where I could possibly be going with bunches of geranium leaves, bundles of lemongrass, and bushels of unripe plums.

I'm not sure of the exact day that I made my first gazoz, but it all happened very organically. I had the idea to make drinks that capitalized on Tel Aviv's rich history of bubbly drinks, which to me felt very much a representation of the city I loved: sunny, communal, social, and

brimming with nature wherever I looked. I started by layering fruit with sugar in jars, then—because I was located smack in the middle of the city's greatest spice market—began suspending cloves, allspice berries, and dried chiles in simple syrup.

Ever since I began making gazoz, I have marveled at its ability to stop people in their tracks. The sheer beauty of the drink itself is a conversation starter—or, truth be told, a conversation stopper, as people tend to be rendered speechless by the sight of a flower-tipped, fruit-filled drink catching and redirecting light beams in every direction. It's a flight of fancy that is eminently doable, utterly enchanting, and undeniably delicious.

GAZOZ AND THE CITY

Gazoz and the city of Tel Aviv have a long, beautiful shared history. Founded in 1909 out of a series of sand dunes, modern Tel Aviv quickly became dotted with kiosks that sold bubbly drinks combining carbonated water with syrups, which were often artificially colored and sweetened. In the early days of Israel, gazoz was as much a social construct as a beverage in a new city bubbling with life and promise.

According to Israeli food journalist Ronit Vered's research, Israel's first seltzer factories sprung up in Jaffa in the 1800s. The first kiosk on Tel Aviv's iconic Rothschild Boulevard, which opened in 1909, sold gazoz. Many others followed suit. Customers would approach a counter and order a glass of seltzer, then point to the flavor of syrup they wanted added to their drink. Similar to an American soda shop, many cafés had a soda apparatus built right into the counter, allowing the proprietor to pull a glass of fresh, cold seltzer on demand.

Soon poets and writers became engaged with this most social of drinks, and gazoz became the inspiration for numerous songs and jingles, such as when legendary poet Haim Nahman Bialik rhymed, "*Gazzezini ve'egrashech, ha'adifini me'meliech*," which loosely translates to, "Sell me a glass of gazoz, and you'll give me change in words."

The writer Yizhar Smilansky, who went by S. Yizhar, also wrote about gazoz:

And the man in the apron takes the tall bright glass in this hand, and in that hand takes the bottle of magic and pours into the glass a measure of red juice, or green or yellow, and when the right amount is reached he turns the glass to the shiny spigot, and into it gushes a torrent of gazoz, and he would raise and lower the glass towards the spigot as if showing off the secrets of his magic. With the flourish of an artist he sets the full glass on the marble countertop, and gives it the slightest push towards the astonished and enchanted customer, who is speechless and even forgets to rummage in his pocket for the half *grush* [coin].

Half a century later, in the late 1970s, an Israeli pop supergroup named Gazoz even had several hits.

Meanwhile, dozens of seltzer home delivery services all over Israel did strong business until the 1970s and '80s. SodaStream, a British company that had been selling seltzer-making machines for the home since its founding in 1903, became very popular in Israel in the 1980s, and was sold to an Israeli entrepreneur in the late 1980s. He increased the apparatus's popularity worldwide to the point where PepsiCo purchased the company for $3.2 billion in 2018. The machines are still proudly manufactured by a multicultural group of Jews and Arabs in Southern Israel.

In recent years, trendy restaurants in Israel and beyond have begun to serve gazoz again. Miznon, a chain of pita sandwich restaurants that originated in Tel Aviv, always has two flavors available, such as apple and apricot, and their branches in cities like New York, Sydney, and Paris all serve gazoz. In Brooklyn, the restaurant Golda serves gazoz in flavors like apple-ginger and matcha. The sparkling drink trend is finding footing all over the world. No matter where you live, it's easy to enjoy gazoz.

How to Use This Book

This book will show you how to create the magic of gazoz in your own kitchen. From fermenting fruit in sugar to brewing probiotic drinks and garnishing your glasses, everything you need is right here among these pages.

By layering elements—sweet and spicy, supple and crisp, fresh and fermented—you will mix up a drink like nothing you've ever had before. You will learn how to build jars of fermented fruits, spices, and chiles. There's information on how to make indulgent syrups using nut butters and tahini that you'll find yourself dipping into again and again. You will get an easy primer on the world of fermented beverages and come out the other side knowing how to make my three favorites—kombucha, jun, and kefir—and get a few suggestions on how to incorporate them into your drinks. And then: the drinks themselves! I will provide you with all the essential steps (as well as useful tips and tricks) to make the dozens of gazoz combinations shown in these pages—not to mention the thousands you can dream up with a little imagination. You make the magic by bringing your own energy, creativity, and style to the glass.

EQUIPMENT

The beauty of gazoz is how few things you actually need to make the drink. There aren't many items you won't already have in your home, and everything else is easy to find in stores or online so you can get yourself started.

Fermentation Equipment

FABRIC

Though I usually just use clean, breathable natural fabric that I cut to size and secure with a rubber band, you can find all manner of cloth jar caps with sewn-in elastic to cover your fermentation jars. The fabric protects the contents of the jar from the elements, keeping out bugs and dust while allowing oxygen in, which promotes the growth of bacteria needed to produce jun, kefir, and kombucha.

GLASS JARS AND BOTTLES

While glass bottles and jars are my vessels of choice for gazoz ingredients, I am not precious about their origin. The truth is, any jar with a sealing lid will do; these can easily be recycled vessels that you've emptied, washed and dried, and saved for just this purpose. The rule is, if you twist it shut and you feel it lock into its grooves, you're in good shape. Try to use containers whose tops haven't rusted and that have a good seal. If you start looking,

you'll notice that some jars
have a rubbery coating inside
the lid, which is a good thing.
Some canning jars come with
what is called a gasket—a flat,
removeable rubber ring that
helps create a tight seal.

KNIFE

A small chef's knife with a
stable handle or a paring knife
are great tools for cutting
produce and trimming herbs.
No need for anything fancy
here; what you already have
in the house is just fine.

ORGANIC PAPER TOWELS

I like to add an extra
layer of protection atop
my fermentation jars to
discourage bugs and pests
from getting too close.
Try Seventh Generation
unbleached paper towels,
which are available in
many grocery stores and on
Amazon.

PERMANENT MARKER

Use a waterproof permanent
marker such as a Sharpie to
label your jars and bottles.

RUBBER BANDS

I use rubber bands to secure
the fabric on top of my
fermentation jars. I don't
think I've ever bought one
in my life; just save all those
newspaper rubber bands and
assorted others—they'll come
in handy here!

SCALE

A simple digital or analog
scale will make quick work
of measuring sugar, produce,
herbs, and spices.

TAPE

Masking tape and painter's
tape are both good for labeling
fermentation jars and bottles
of syrup with their contents
and date of production.

Gazoz-Making Equipment

FINE-MESH STRAINERS
These are great for straining kefir grains (see page 68) from their fermentation liquid or straining sweet fermented fruit from syrup.

GLASSES
This is the main stage for your drink, so make sure you put your best one forward. A tall, clear glass between 14 and 16 ounces (415 to 475 ml) in volume is ideal for the job, and will showcase your creation perfectly.

LONG-HANDLED SPOON
A bar spoon, typically used for mixing cocktails, is perfect for mixing gazoz. If you don't have one, use a dinner knife or a grilling skewer.

PEELER
I use a simple Y-style peeler to create thin strips of fruits and vegetables, but a sharp kitchen knife works well if you don't have one.

REUSABLE STRAWS
Reusable straws are sustainable and attractive. You can find glass, metal, bamboo, and silicone versions at housewares stores and online. Standard straws work nicely, but wider straws— about 1/3 inch (1 cm) in width—are a whimsical touch that also make it possible to suck up small pieces of fruit.

Sweet
Fermentation

THE FIRST THING that draws people to my shop is the sight of beautiful jars of fruits and spices, a visual jewel box right before their very eyes. Countless people have discovered gazoz for the first time merely because of the visual appeal of these gorgeous clear vessels displaying their precious materials. I like to think of this collection as nature's display case, one that inspires and intrigues as it promises a flavorful future.

Fermenting the raw materials for gazoz, an elemental component of virtually every glass, is a simple and satisfying ritual I undertake almost daily. Layering peak-season fruit with simple white sugar and leaving it alone draws some of the fruit's juices out (a process known as maceration), creating a delicate syrup that serves as the sweetening agent for gazoz (or as a treat all of its own). The fruit is the lifeblood of the drink, the ingredient that anchors every glass to a season. A persimmon, a pear, a peach—each speaks to a different moment in the year and to the ephemeral nature of sun and soil. The fruit captures the moment and anchors the glass.

After a day or two, the fruit begins to ferment, lending complexity and depth of flavor. Because they are deprived of oxygen, my fruits progress very quickly to the alcoholic stage of fermentation that occurs when they come into contact with airborne natural yeasts. This is known as anaerobic fermentation; the absence of oxygen in the sealed jars accelerates the process.

Clockwise, from top left: plums in the middle of their sweet fermentation; jars of fruit ready to be incorporated into glasses of gazoz; citron fruit (*etrog* in Hebrew) macerating in simple syrup; sweet-fermented Persian limes, Scotch bonnet peppers, and hibiscus-tinged clementines

SWEET FERMENTED FRUIT IN SYRUP

Start the fermentation process with clean, unblemished fruit of the highest quality, preferably organic, seasonal, and local. The fruit is the star of the show and should be treated as such, especially because once you're done drinking your gazoz, you will most likely lift the juicy slices of fruit out of the glass and eat them. The general rule for the fruit-to-sugar ratio is 70 percent sugar in relation to the weight of the fruit. Use that as your guide, unless otherwise indicated.

MAKES 3 TO 4 CUPS (ABOUT 1 KG) FRUIT WITH SYRUP

1 heaping tablespoon (20 g) baking soda

1¾ pounds (800 g) whole thin-skinned fruit (see Notes)

Lemon juice (optional)

1¼ pounds (560 grams) sugar

1. **Wash the fruit:** Combine the baking soda with 2 quarts (2 l) cold water in a large bowl; add the fruit, rub it well with a soft cloth to clean it, then transfer it to a separate large bowl filled with ice water; let the fruit stand for 30 minutes to firm up.

2. **Prepare the fruit:** Slice the fruit into 1-inch (2.5 cm) wedges (remove the cores, stems, and pits); you should end up with about 1½ pounds (700 g) cut fruit. If you're using fruits that might turn brown (such as apples, pears, quince, etc.), drop them in a bowl filled with a mixture of 90 percent water to 10 percent lemon juice as you slice them.

3. **Layer some of the fruit** in a roughly 1-quart (1 l) jar with a tight-fitting lid, then

28 GAZOZ

Santa Rosa plums in three stages of sweet fermentation (*left to right*): fresh and mixed with sugar; midway through their transformation (about one week); and finished with their sweet fermentation (about 2 weeks)

sprinkle with sugar. Continue to layer the fruit and sugar until the jar is filled, leaving at least 1½ inches of headroom at the top of the jar.

4. **Ferment the fruit:** Seal the jar tightly and let it stand on the counter until a syrup has formed and the fruit has softened and slumped slightly, 1 to 3 days, depending on the temperature of your kitchen; the sugar will dissolve more with each passing day. Open the jars daily to release any built-up pressure from fermentation, and also to check the progress of the fruit. This is the critical juncture; once you detect an aroma that is the essence of the fruit with a drop

of sourness and acidity—sort of like cider—
that is the time to decide if you want to let
it ferment longer so it becomes more tart, or
refrigerate the jar to slow fermentation. You
can also dip a spoon in to taste the syrup,
which will give you a good indication of
what's going on in the jar.

5. When you are happy with the flavor of
the fruit, transfer the jar to the refrigerator.
Use the fermented fruit and its syrup within
2 weeks.

» **Notes:** To make 1¾ pounds (800 g) whole fruit, you'll need 4 or 5 apples,
peaches, or pears, or 8 to 10 plums or apricots.

If using fresh berries, omit steps 1 and 2.

A WORD ABOUT MOLD, SPOILAGE, AND INSECTS

Since you are dealing with fresh produce, mold—grown from tiny spores that attach to food, creating a chemical reaction that causes food to spoil— is inevitable. I view mold as part of what I do, part of the cycle of life. Of course, certain kinds of mold—black and green in particular—indicate that food may have developed some harmful properties, and in most cases, that food should be discarded. But if I see a small amount of white mold at the edge of a jar (similar to seeing some snowy residue on the outer reaches of a wedge of Parmigiano Reggiano), I will often wipe it away and carry on. Mold is not the kiss of death for a jar of fermented fruit; you just need to use your best judgment. Of course, when in doubt, throw it out—but not in every instance. If you discover worms or bugs, though, chuck that batch and start fresh!

FERMENTED WHOLE DRIED SPICES AND CHILES

Adding the flavor of spices and chiles to beverages opens up new worlds of flavor. Think of the way the addition of black pepper, cloves, or chiles enhances savory food—or even desserts—and you get the picture. There really are no rules for how you combine flavors, but use a light touch when adding these quick-change artists to your glass of gazoz.

Spices and chiles contain essential oils that dissipate over time, so the fresher the spices, the fresher the oils. When combined with simple syrup, their flavors meld to create the optimal finished product. If you're using cloves, for instance, inhale deeply; the aroma should almost overwhelm you, a veritable spice bazaar under your nose. Try to get whole, not broken, spices, and make sure there is no sand, bugs, or anything else that shouldn't be there.

Cinnamon sticks; whole cardamom pods; allspice berries; black, green, or pink peppercorns—any whole dried spice you would want to grind to season your food will work wonderfully here—as well as dried chiles.

(recipe continues)

MAKES 1 CUP (240 ML)

1. Place the spices or chiles in a clean
6-ounce (180 ml) jar with a tight-fitting lid,
leaving about an inch (2.5 cm) of headroom.

1¾ ounces (60 g)
whole dried spices, or
½ ounce (15 g) dried
hot chiles, such as
chile de árbol

2. Carefully pour the simple syrup on
top of the spices or chiles, making sure the
spices or chiles are completely covered.

¾ cup (180 ml)
1:1 Simple Syrup
(page 46), at room
temperature, plus
more as needed

3. Seal the jar tightly and rinse the outside
with warm water to remove any sticky
syrup; dry.

4. Let stand at room temperature for at
least 1 week before using, adding more
simple syrup to cover the spices or chiles
as they absorb the liquid, so the flavors
really infuse into the syrup. The spices or
chiles will keep at room temperature for at
least a year. (If you're going on a trip and
your house will be left warm without air-
conditioning while you're gone, pop the jars
in the refrigerator until you return.)

SPICES IDEAL FOR SWEET FERMENTATION

The Levinsky Market area in Tel Aviv, where I live and work—and home to some of Israel's most famous spice shops—inspires the ever-growing list of spices I like to preserve and use in my drinks. As in cooking, using the freshest, best spices you can get your hands on is vital here; you'll taste the difference in the intensity of the syrups they produce.

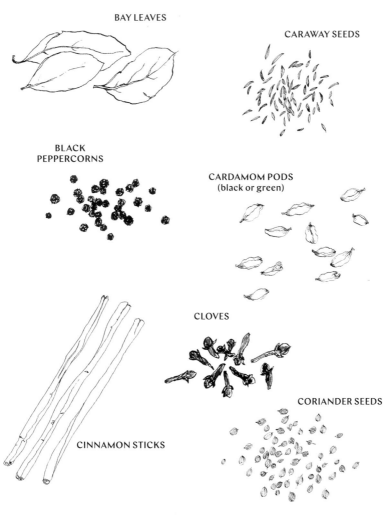

BAY LEAVES

CARAWAY SEEDS

BLACK
PEPPERCORNS

CARDAMOM PODS
(black or green)

CLOVES

CORIANDER SEEDS

CINNAMON STICKS

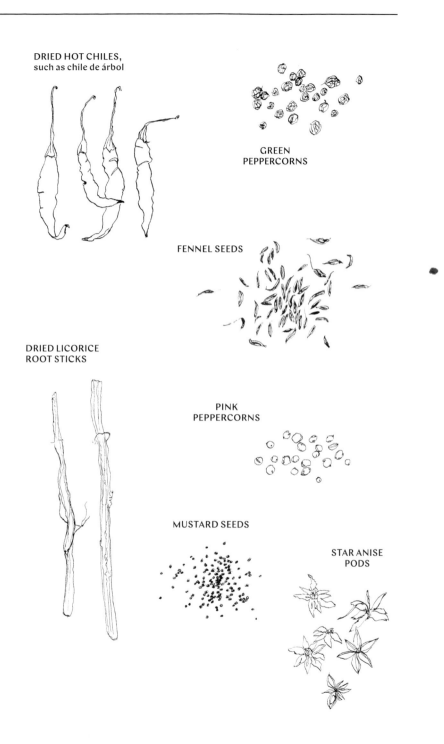

DRIED HOT CHILES,
such as chile de árbol

GREEN
PEPPERCORNS

FENNEL SEEDS

DRIED LICORICE
ROOT STICKS

PINK
PEPPERCORNS

MUSTARD SEEDS

STAR ANISE
PODS

Fruit and Vegetable Juice Syrups and Flavored Simple Syrups

NO MATTER WHAT THE SEASON, you can capture the essence of fresh produce in a bottle or jar. In some cases, the raw materials lend themselves more easily to a syrup than to macerating the fruits themselves. This method works particularly well with vegetables, which, in their solid form, are often less appropriate for adorning a glass of gazoz.

FRUIT AND VEGETABLE JUICE SYRUPS

A juice hued a vibrant pink, jade green, or sunny orange adds cheery color and flavor intrigue to the glass. These syrups are easy to make, and thanks to the sugar, which acts as a preservative, they will keep in the refrigerator for a good 2 weeks.

Watermelon Syrup

2.2 pounds (1 kg) ripe watermelon flesh, preferably seedless

½ cup (100 g) sugar

Similar to cucumber, watermelon is composed almost entirely of water, which lends itself to easy juicing.

MAKES 1½ CUPS (360 ML)

Puree the watermelon in a blender or food processor until smooth, then strain the puree through a fine-mesh strainer into a bowl; discard the pulp and seeds (or discard the seeds and use the pulp in a smoothie). Add the sugar and whisk until it has dissolved. Transfer to an airtight bottle or jar and store in the refrigerator until ready to use. It will keep for up to 2 weeks.

Cucumber Syrup

Grate the cucumber by hand with the peel on, which lends a lovely deeper green hue to the juice. The skins can be a bit bitter, but thankfully, the sugar takes care of that.

MAKES 1½ CUPS (360 ML)

Grate the cucumbers on the large holes of a box grater or in a food processor using the shredding disc (see Note). Place the grated cucumber in the center of a clean kitchen towel, fold the ends over the cucumber, then squeeze as much juice as you can into a bowl; you should have about 1 cup (240 ml) juice. Discard the solids, or reserve them for tzatziki or another use. Add the sugar and whisk until dissolved. Transfer the syrup to an airtight bottle or jar and store in the refrigerator until ready to use. It will keep for up to 2 weeks.

2.2 pounds (1 kg) firm cucumbers, preferably Persian

½ cup (100 g) sugar

» **Note:** You can puree the cucumber instead of grating it, then strain it, but the juice will be slightly more bitter. Place the cucumber in a food processor or blender and puree, then transfer to a fine-mesh strainer set over a bowl. Gently push against the solids using a wooden spoon or silicone spatula to extract all the juice.

Tomato Syrup

MAKES 2 CUPS (480 ML)

Set a fine-mesh strainer over a bowl. Hand-grate the tomatoes on the large holes of a box grater into the strainer, then press down on the solids with a wooden spoon or silicone spatula; you should end up with 1 cup (240 ml) tomato juice (reserve the solids for a pasta or pizza sauce). Add the sugar and whisk until it has dissolved. Transfer the syrup to an airtight bottle or jar and store in the refrigerator until ready to use. It will keep for up to 2 weeks.

2.2 pounds (1 kg) ripe, juicy medium or large tomatoes, such as vine-ripened or Roma (plum)

½ cup (100 g) sugar

Beet or Carrot Syrup

Thanks to Israel's fresh juice culture, I have access to fresh-pressed juice from local stands whenever I have the desire to drink it or make it into a syrup. If you don't have a juicer, you can buy cold-pressed juices from a juice shop or local market; shelf-stable pure juices will work well, too—just know the color and flavor of your syrup may not be quite as bright as with fresh.

1 cup (240 ml) fresh beet or carrot juice

½ cup (100 g) sugar

MAKES 1½ CUPS (360 ML)

Combine the beet or carrot juice and the sugar in a medium bowl and whisk until the sugar has dissolved. Transfer to an airtight bottle or jar and store in the refrigerator until ready to use. It will keep for up to 2 weeks.

Left to right: tomato, beet, and carrot syrups

FRESH GINGER AND TURMERIC PUREES

To give gazoz a flavor zing—not to mention an antioxidant boost—add a small amount of fresh ginger or turmeric puree to the glass. As an alternative to homemade puree, you can purchase fresh ginger or turmeric juice "shots" in tiny bottles at juice shops, health food stores and markets, and some supermarkets (see Shopping Guide, page 203). Experiment with the strength you like to add to your gazoz, but aim for somewhere between ½ teaspoon and 1 teaspoon of either puree or store-bought juice.

MAKES ½ CUP (120 ML)

3½ ounces (100 g) fresh ginger or turmeric

Peel the ginger or turmeric (see Note) and transfer it to the small bowl of a food processor or a bullet-style blender. Process or blend until smooth; add a drop of water if needed to facilitate blending. Store in an airtight container in the refrigerator for up to 2 months.

» **Note:** Wear gloves when working with raw turmeric if you don't want it to stain your hands yellow.

Turmeric (*foreground*) and ginger (*background*) purees

FLAVORED SIMPLE SYRUPS

These delicious, versatile syrups are no more complicated than a 1:1 Simple Syrup recipe, but they're infused with a variety of special ingredients. Unlike fermented spices, here the tables are turned: the simple syrup is the star. I provide three actual recipes, but the possibilities are endless and only limited by the reaches of your imagination. These syrups are meant to add a hint of flavor to a gazoz and would be equally good mixed into a cocktail, stirred into a cup of hot tea, or drizzled lightly over fresh fruit or cake.

1:1 Simple Syrup

1½ cups (300 g) sugar

1½ cups (320 ml) water

Wherever straightforward simple syrup is called for, this is the recipe to use. I follow a very basic 1:1 ratio of sugar to water. Use it to ferment spices and mix it with fruit and vegetable juices. It plays well with anything you mix it with, is neither treacly nor watery, and can be made in less than 5 minutes. Stored in an airtight container in the refrigerator, simple syrup keeps indefinitely.

MAKES 2 CUPS (480 ML)

Combine the sugar and water in a small saucepan and bring to a low boil over medium heat, stirring occasionally. Boil just until the sugar has dissolved, then reduce the heat to very low and simmer for 1 to 2 minutes. Let cool completely, then transfer to an airtight container and store in the refrigerator until ready to use.

Citrus Flower Syrup

If you have a relationship with a citrus grower, ask them to save you some blossoms. You can also find dried pure orange flower petals online, or just use orange flower water or orange oil, which are easier to find.

MAKES 2 CUPS (480 ML)

Combine the simple syrup and citrus blossoms in an airtight bottle or jar. Seal and refrigerate until ready to use. After 2 weeks, strain off the flowers; it will keep for up to 6 months refrigerated.

2 cups (480 ml) 1:1 Simple Syrup (page 46)

A few fresh citrus blossoms, or 3 drops of orange flower water or orange oil (see Shopping Guide, page 203)

¼ cup (18 g) thinly sliced strips of citrus peel

Vanilla Bean Syrup

MAKES 2 CUPS (480 ML)

Combine the simple syrup, vanilla bean pod, and vanilla seeds in an airtight bottle or jar. Seal and refrigerate until ready to use. It will keep for up to 1 year.

2 cups (480 ml)
1:1 Simple Syrup
(page 46)

1 vanilla bean, split lengthwise and seeds scraped out

Truffle Syrup

MAKES 2 CUPS (480 ML)

Combine the simple syrup and truffle in an airtight bottle or jar. Seal and refrigerate until ready to use. It will keep for up to 6 months.

2 cups (480 ml)
1:1 Simple Syrup
(page 46)

1 teaspoon shaved white or black truffle or truffle oil

Fermented Medjool Dates and Syrup

MAKES 1 CUP (240 ML)

Combine the simple syrup and dates in a jar. Seal tightly and let sit at room temperature until the dates soften slightly, 3 to 4 days, then refrigerate until ready to use. It will keep for up to 6 months.

1 cup (240 ml)
1:1 Simple Syrup
(page 46)

4 Medjool dates, halved and pitted

Left to right: vanilla bean, pomelo blossom, and truffle syrups

Rose Petal Syrup

Most varieties of rose petals are edible! Check before you pick them (or purchase food-grade unsprayed rose petals).

MAKES 1 CUP (240 L)

Soak the rose petals in cold water to cover for 10 minutes, changing the water every 2 to 3 minutes, to remove any thorns or dirt. Drain the petals, leaving about 1 tablespoon water. Transfer the petals to a bowl and sprinkle with the lemon juice, tossing lightly to coat (this helps remove the tannins from the petals). Let the rose petals sit in the lemon juice for a few hours, then sprinkle with the sugar and let stand at room temperature, stirring every few hours, until the sugar has dissolved, 24 hours. Transfer to a jar, seal, and store in the refrigerator for up to 1 year (see Note).

3 cups (130 to 150 g) edible food-grade fresh rose petals

2 tablespoons fresh lemon juice

¼ cup (50 g) sugar

» **Note:** If you'd like to sterilize the syrup before storage, transfer the mixture to a small saucepan and simmer over low heat for 3 minutes; remove from the heat and let cool completely, then store as directed.

MILKSHAKE SYRUPS AND GAZOZ

I like to call these the "B sides" to my fruitier drinks.
When mixed with seltzer and made creamy, these
luxurious drinks are reminiscent of milkshakes in their
richness. Usually no more than pure nut paste blended
with sugar and boiling water, milkshake syrups are
so simple to make, it's almost laughable. They lend a
cloudy mystique to a glass of gazoz, plus a richness
you typically achieve only with the addition of dairy
products.

Left to right: peanut
butter, pistachio,
chocolate, nigella
(or black sesame),
halvah (tahini), and
pumpkin seed syrups

MAKING NUT BUTTERS

You can make your own nut butters at home. A high-speed blender like a Vitamix or Blendtec makes easy work of the process, but a food processor or standard blender will work as well, though it will take longer and you may need to add a drop of neutral oil to loosen the nut butter initially. I would not recommend making black or white sesame seed butters at home; the amount of time and power needed to liquefy the sesame seeds raises their temperature so much that the resulting "tahini" can become bitter.

To make nut butters from pistachios, peanuts, walnuts, hazelnuts, and almonds, start with 2 cups (240 to 260 g, depending on the nuts) blanched, unroasted nuts and pulse them in the blender or food processor until finely chopped. Turn the blender or food processor on high and process, stopping to scrape down the bowl if necessary, until smooth, 2 to 3 minutes.

Peanut Butter, Pistachio, Nigella (or Black Sesame), Halvah (Tahini), or Pumpkin Seed Syrup

MAKES 2 CUPS (480 ML)

¾ cup (200 g) smooth all-natural nut butter, seed butter, or tahini (see page 53 or Shopping Guide, page 203)

1 cup (200 g) sugar

1 cup (240 ml) boiling water

In a large bowl, whisk together the nut butter, sugar, and boiling water until the sugar has dissolved and the mixture is smooth. Let cool to room temperature (if desired, strain through a fine-mesh strainer and discard any nut particles), then transfer to an airtight bottle or jar and refrigerate until ready to use. It will keep for up to 3 months.

Chocolate Syrup

MAKES 2 CUPS (480 ML)

6 ounces (200 g) good-quality bittersweet or milk chocolate, coarsely chopped

⅔ cup (160 ml) boiling water

⅔ cup (160 ml) 1:1 Simple Syrup (page 46)

In a large bowl, whisk together the chocolate, boiling water, and simple syrup until smooth and pourable. Transfer to an airtight glass jar or bottle and seal. Store in the refrigerator until ready to use. It will keep for up to 3 months.

» **Note:** Though they may appear like black sesame seeds from a distance, look closer and you'll see that nigella seeds resemble tiny rough-hewn stones. A member of the onion family, they taste vaguely of alliums and nothing like sesame at all. However, they can be used interchangeably, especially in savory preparations.

EGG CREAM

This recipe was introduced to me by my coauthor, Adeena Sussman, who grew up drinking this American soda-fountain classic.

1½ ounces (45 ml) Chocolate Syrup (page 54)

3 ounces (90 ml) milk of your choice (dairy or nondairy)

6 ounces (175 ml) chilled seltzer

Pour the chocolate syrup into a tall glass, add the milk, then top with the seltzer. Stir to your desired level of smoothness.

JUN
28.04.19

Kombucha, Jun, and Kefir

PART OF A TRADITION of fermented beverages that dates back thousands of years, kombucha (from China), jun (from Korea), and kefir (believed to hail from the Caucasus in the former Soviet Union) are health-promoting, delicious beverages. They are an excellent addition to gazoz or can be served on their own—and more and more people are seeking out their distinctive sweet-tangy flavor profile and health benefits.

Making these drinks reminds me that a wild energy informs every step of the process. You never quite know what will happen when bacteria react with sugar, time, and varying amounts of oxygen deprivation. I marvel every day at how every batch comes out a little different based on a variety of conditions: the temperature of the location where it's made, the particular macrobacteria in the environment, and the hardiness of the bacterial element, or SCOBY (see next page), you're using.

There have been many more-scientific guides written about these drinks and how to make them, but my goal is to encourage you to feel comfortable with the process without getting *too* caught up in the science. With a little bit of knowledge and some very basic equipment, you can enjoy a full complement of tasty drinks in your home, with endless flavor permutations—all at a fraction of the cost of buying them at the store.

The critical element in both jun and kombucha is a SCOBY (symbiotic culture of bacteria and yeast), which, in combination with tea and sugar, enables and accelerates fermentation. Jellylike and floppy, a SCOBY is made up mostly of cellulose, a food-grade soluble fiber. Kind of like a giant mushroom, the SCOBY contains bacteria that coax sugar along on its journey to the signature tart acidity that gives kombucha and jun their unique taste. The best part is that since SCOBYs regenerate on their own, you will be self-supplied for years . . . and be able to pay it forward by sharing SCOBYs with friends and family with enough left over for yourself. You can easily find kombucha and jun SCOBYs in health food stores and online (see Shopping

Guide, page 203). They will come stored in what is called "starter tea," which is essentially kombucha or jun used to keep the SCOBY fresh and active.

The process of tending to kombucha, kefir, and jun (and their respective SCOBYs and grains) is like making and keeping a sourdough mother going; with the right attention, they can produce delicious beverages for years.

These fermented drinks all contain probiotics in the form of *Lactobacillus*, "good" bacteria believed to encourage gut health and digestion. For any of the drinks in this book, make a half-and-half gazoz by swapping out half the seltzer for some single-fermented kombucha, jun, or kefir.

KOMBUCHA

Hailing from China, kombucha generally is made from black tea with added granulated sugar to initiate fermentation. I use green tea rather than black, as I like the mellower results and delicate flavor. Use the best quality green tea leaves you can find, preferably whole, unbroken leaves that have a deep green color and a lovely fragrance.

MAKES 12 CUPS (3 L)

½ ounce (15 g) pure green tea leaves

3½ ounces (100 g) sugar

2 cups (480 ml) unsweetened raw kombucha (available at health food stores)

1 kombucha SCOBY, from a previous batch of kombucha or store-bought (see Shopping Guide, page 203)

1. Place the tea leaves in a 1-quart (1 l) glass jar or bowl.

2. Bring 4 cups (1 l) of water to a boil, pour it over the tea leaves, and steep for 5 minutes.

3. Strain the liquid into a 3-quart (3 l) glass jar; discard the tea leaves. Add the sugar and stir until it has dissolved.

4. Add 8 cups (2 l) water. Add the kombucha and stir to combine.

5. Place the SCOBY on top of the liquid. Cover the jar with a piece of breathable fabric, top it with a paper towel, and secure with a rubber band. Store at room temperature out of direct sunlight for 2 weeks.

6. After 2 weeks, remove the cloth and let the aroma from the jar reach your nose; the kombucha should smell like something between apple cider and apple cider vinegar.

(recipe continues)

Taste a teaspoon of the liquid; it should be balanced between sweet, tart, and slightly fermented. If it isn't, cover the jar and let it ferment for 3 to 5 days more, then check again. Note that the warmer the weather (or the temperature in your home), the faster the kombucha will be ready; the colder it is, the more time it will take.

7. Remove the SCOBY and place it in an airtight container; pour over 1 cup (240 ml) of the kombucha. Store in the refrigerator indefinitely to use for future batches of kombucha.

8. Line a fine-mesh strainer with three layers of cheesecloth and set it over a bowl. Strain the kombucha through the strainer, then decant it into 1-quart (1 l) bottles, seal, and refrigerate. The kombucha will keep for up to 1 month; open the bottles every 2 days during storage to release pressure.

JUN

Jun differs from kombucha in that it uses honey in place of sugar at the beginning of the fermentation process.

MAKES 12 CUPS (3 L)

1. Place the tea leaves in a 1-quart (1 l) glass jar or bowl.

2. Bring 4 cups (1 l) water to a boil, pour it over the tea leaves, and steep for 5 minutes.

3. Strain the liquid into a 3-quart (3 l) glass jar; discard the tea leaves. Add the honey and stir until it has dissolved.

4. Add 8 cups (2 l) water.

5. Place the SCOBY on top of the liquid. Cover the jar with a piece of breathable fabric, top it with a paper towel, and secure with a rubber band. Store at room temperature out of direct sunlight for 10 days.

6. After 10 to 14 days (depending on the weather), remove the cloth and let the aroma from the jar reach your nose; the jun should smell less acidic than kombucha, but still have a discernable acidity. Taste a teaspoon of the liquid; it should be balanced between sweet, tart, and slightly fermented. If it isn't, cover the jar and let ferment 3 to 5 days more, then check again. Note that the warmer the weather (or the temperature in

½ ounce (15 g) pure green tea leaves

7 ounces (200 g) honey (preferably raw), or a little more to taste

1 jun SCOBY, homemade (see page 203) or store-bought (see Shopping Guide, page 203)

your home), the faster the jun will be ready; the colder it is, the more time it will take.

7. Remove the SCOBY and place it in an airtight container; pour over 1 cup (240 ml) of the jun. Store in the refrigerator indefinitely to use for future batches of jun.

8. Line a fine-mesh strainer with three layers of cheesecloth and set it over a bowl. Strain the jun through the strainer, then decant it into 1-quart (1 l) bottles, seal, and refrigerate. The jun will keep in the refrigerator for up to 1 month; open the bottles every 2 days during storage to release pressure.

Jun, fermenting with its SCOBY

GAZOZ

KEFIR

Water kefir is milder and mellower in taste and lower in acidity than kombucha and jun. The drink starts with opaque, quivering jewel-like beads known as water kefir grains made from cultured bacteria and yeast. I always begin with water kefir so that my drinks remain dairy-free and vegan. You can easily find water kefir grains in health food stores and online (see Shopping Guide, page 203). Since kefir is milder, integrate it into gazoz that has stronger flavors, like fig gazoz (see page 193).

MAKES 4 CUPS (1 L)

4 cups (1 l) cold water

¼ cup (50 g) sugar

3½ ounces (100 g) water kefir grains (see headnote)

4 slices fresh fruit of your choice (plums, apples, pears, peaches; see page 70)

1. Combine 1 cup (240 ml) of the water and the sugar in a 5- or 6-cup (1,200 to 1,340 ml) jar or bowl; stir to dissolve the sugar.

2. Add the remaining 3 cups (760 ml) water, then add the kefir grains.

3. Cover the jar or bowl with a piece of breathable fabric, top it with a paper towel, and secure them with a rubber band. Store out of direct sunlight for 18 hours.

4. Pour the liquid through a fine-mesh strainer set over a jar or bowl. Transfer the kefir grains to an airtight container and store in the refrigerator for 3 weeks to use for future batches of kefir.

5. Transfer the kefir to a 1-quart (1 l) bottle and add the fruit. Seal tightly.

6. Let the kefir sit on the counter until bubbles begin to form, 2 to 3 days, then transfer the bottle to the refrigerator. The kefir will keep for up to 2 weeks; open the bottle every day or two during storage to release pressure.

The kefir-making process, including the second fermentation (*see next page*)

SECOND FERMENTATION

Once you've brewed your kombucha, jun, or kefir, you can do what is called a second fermentation, if you'd like. Simply add a few slices of the fruit of your choice to the bottle (or bottles) and let it sit on the counter for a few days, until you see bubbles or hear carbonation when you open the bottle or the cap of the bottle or jar is slightly puffed. Refrigerate, opening the bottle every day or two to release carbonation. Drink within a week. Adding fruit supercharges the process and introduces bubbles quickly because of the extra sugar, so if you're a fan of the fizz, this is something you'll want to do. Red plums work particularly well, since they lend both vibrant color and a delicate, fruity flavor to the drink.

Edible and Food-Grade Flowers and Greens

THERE'S A WHOLE world of flora and fauna just waiting to be added to the top of your gazoz. One of the greatest pleasures of building a glass is decorating it with leaves, herbs, greens, and flowers, which lend both visual appeal and, often, a heady scent of nature. Your choices can be as simple as a basil leaf or as involved as an edible array of citrus flowers, geranium leaves, and wildflowers that you either forage, pick, or buy. Unlike fruit, which is more readily available, you may have to dig a little deeper to pinpoint the most special toppers, like a pomelo flower. The first step is to open your eyes and your olfactory nerves; chances are, if you don't have a garden yourself, you have a neighbor or friend who does. People who grow things are generally thrilled to share them, so ask them to alert you when the citrus blossoms appear on their trees, or alert your local greengrocer that rather than throwing away his beet greens after trimming them off their bulbs, you'd love it if he saved them for you. I encourage you to explore becoming a forager yourself. Buy a book or two (see Reading Resources, page 205), or take a course that gets you out of the house and into nature. You'll learn what's edible or food-grade (lemongrass, for instance, isn't edible in a gazoz, but you should by all means use it for its enticing aroma and for the drama a long stalk adds to the glass as a garnish).

Many people are unaware of just how many of the fruits we love to eat grow from fragrant—and edible—flowers and blossoms. In addition to being incredibly romantic symbols of love, fertility, and possibility—not to mention magical in appearance—flowers represent an entire world unto themselves and are equally appealing in a gazoz.

EDIBLE FLOWERS AND HERBS

The list of edible flowers and herbs could be as long as this book. Some of these flowers, such as nasturtiums, are packaged like produce and sold at gourmet stores. Others can be purchased at farmers' markets and florists or plucked from your own garden. Just make sure to double-check that you're using an edible, food-grade variety; when in doubt, consult a book (see Reading Resources, page 205).

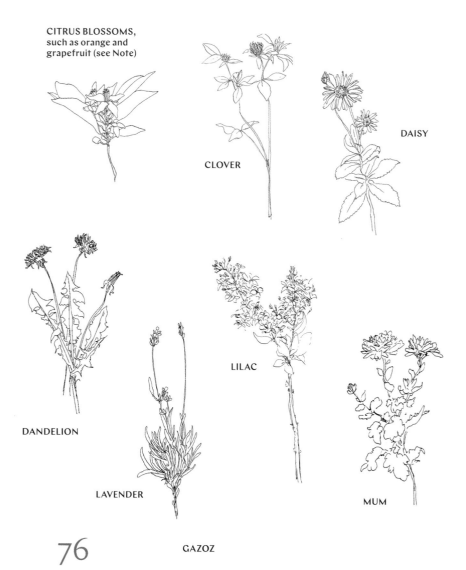

CITRUS BLOSSOMS, such as orange and grapefruit (see Note)

CLOVER

DAISY

DANDELION

LAVENDER

LILAC

MUM

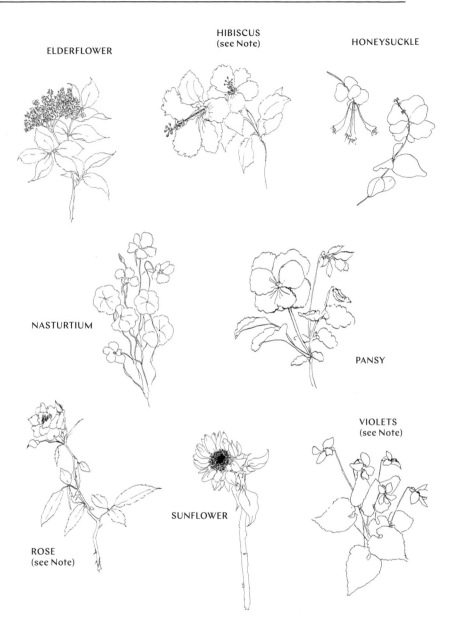

ELDERFLOWER

HIBISCUS
(see Note)

HONEYSUCKLE

NASTURTIUM

PANSY

VIOLETS
(see Note)

ROSE
(see Note)

SUNFLOWER

» **Note:** While I typically use fresh flowers as garnish, some can be suspended in 1:1 syrup (see page 46) to create a sweet floral ferment. Place ½ cup (10 g) dried flowers in a 6-ounce (175 ml) jar, then cover with syrup. Seal tightly, ferment on the counter for 1 week, then refrigerate for up to 1 year.

HERBS

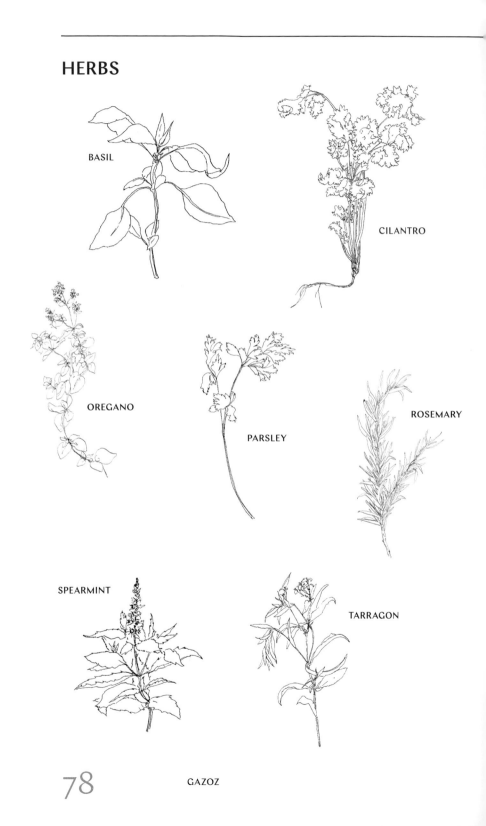

BASIL

CILANTRO

OREGANO

PARSLEY

ROSEMARY

SPEARMINT

TARRAGON

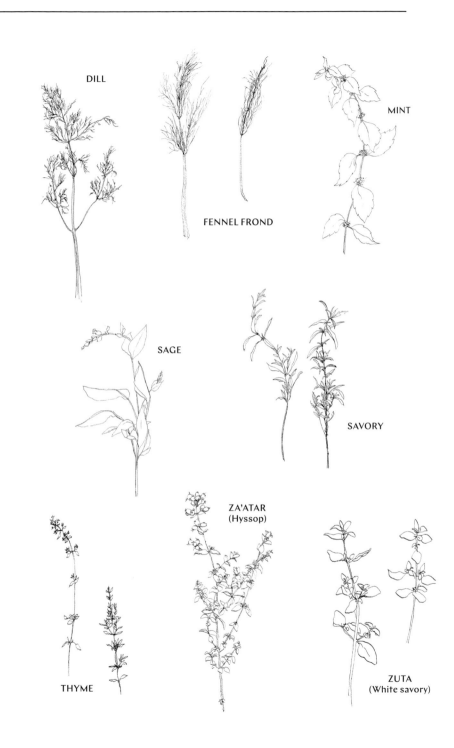

DILL

FENNEL FROND

MINT

SAGE

SAVORY

ZA'ATAR
(Hyssop)

THYME

ZUTA
(White savory)

HOW TO DRINK A GAZOZ

Drinking a gazoz is an experience that, in the best-case scenario, allows you to slow down and enjoy it with all your senses engaged. Here is how I like to do it.

1. Lift the glass and take a look at it; take in its physical beauty, its color, the way it captures nature, the way the bubbles keep the glass in perpetual motion, filled with life.

2. Raise the glass to your nose and inhale the aroma; first the top floral and herbal notes, then the more subtle scents of fruit and spice transported from inside the glass to the atmosphere by the tiny bubbles.

3. Finally, take a sip of the gazoz through a straw. Feel the slight prick of the bubbles on your tongue, the tangy fizz of fermentation, the pleasing sweetness of macerated fruit. Stir, releasing the subtle funk of preservation, then use a spoon to lift a piece of fruit from the glass. Eat the fruit.

4. Repeat.

Gazoz Drinks

NOW THAT YOU'VE learned how to prepare all the components of a delicious glass of gazoz, it's time to make some drinks. All you need is a tall glass, a long spoon (a bar spoon is ideal) for stirring, a straw (preferably glass or metal), and a source of sparkling water—either bottled or one made at home with the aid of a seltzer maker such as a SodaStream. Once you've gathered all four, you're ready to get started.

The perfect glass of gazoz is a balanced creation that integrates all its elements into perfect harmony. Though every glass of gazoz varies, certain elements remain constant. No gazoz leaves my shop without a few slices of macerated fruit and its accompanying syrup at its base, along with a piece of sugar-preserved whole spice or hot chile, plus some fresh herbs and edible flowers. I have come up with a general formula that will guide you in building your glass, but know that you ultimately decide how your glass looks, tastes, and smells. If you like it sweet, add more syrup. Like it tart? Add more kombucha. You get the picture … the most important thing is to feel you have created something that is as beautiful to look at as it is to drink.

The drinks you'll see on the following pages are merely suggestions based on combinations I make at my shop, but there is no end to the combinations you can create if you let creativity be your guide. There are no "incorrect" gazoz, only new recipes waiting to be created.

Basic Gazoz

These are the basic proportions to follow when building a simple gazoz. Master this, and every glass will be your creative playground.

MAKES 1 DRINK

3 or 4 large ice cubes (see Note)

2 slices or pieces of fermented fruit (see page 28), plus 1 to 2 tablespoons syrup from the fruit or milkshake syrup (see page 52)

1 or 2 slices fresh fruit

1 or 2 pieces fermented whole spice or chiles, plus 1 teaspoon fermented spice syrup

12 ounces (355 ml) sparkling water

Leaves, greens, herbs, and flowers of your choice

Place the ice in a 12- to 16-ounce (360 to 475 ml) glass; spoon in the fermented fruit syrup. Add the fermented fruit, fresh fruit, fermented spice, and fermented spice syrup on top. Fill the glass with sparkling water, then garnish the top with the herbs, leaves, greens, and flowers of your choice. Insert straw and drink immediately.

» **Note:** Though any ice cubes work well, cubes made with filtered mineral water or tap water that has been boiled and cooled will be clearer and more compact, and will melt more slowly. Try to avoid crushed ice, which will melt quickly and dilute your beverage.

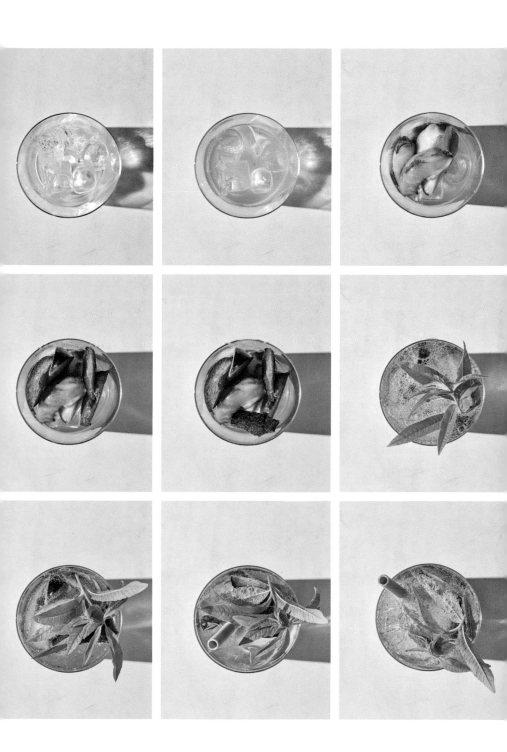

STYLING YOUR GLASS

Every gazoz you make is an opportunity to express your creativity through the way you select, arrange, and present its components. Below are a few tips I've collected over the years to make sure you put your best fizz forward.

1. **Think visually.** Whether you concoct a combination of colors in your glass or opt for a monotone presentation, make sure your gazoz is gorgeous. Half the appeal is that first look: colors, textures, and movement all coming together in a stunning visual.

2. **Make it extra fizzy.** If you are using a home seltzer maker, crank up the carbonation to its highest setting; you'll get prettier bubbles that way.

3. **Don't use too much ice.** Once it starts to melt, it will dilute the colors and flavors of the drink, so go light on those cubes.

4. **Control the top.** Make sure you have enough herbs and flowers to create visual appeal without overwhelming your gazoz.

5. **Straw first.** If you're designing a drink that you want to photograph, put the straw in first! That way, your composition won't be ruined by poking the straw in after everything else is in place.

6. **Vary your glass size.** If you're making a few gazoz drinks for friends, feel free to use a variety of mismatched glasses— different widths, heights, and textures—to create visual intrigue.

STARTER GAZOZ

Peach

Ice

Fermented peach slices
and syrup (see page 28)

Fermented pink peppercorns
and syrup (see page 33)

Basil leaves

Seltzer

Pineapple Mango

Ice

Fresh or fermented pineapple and syrup (see page 28)

Cubed fresh or fermented mango and syrup (see page 28)

Coconut water

Seltzer

Mint sprig, for garnish

Plum Cherry

Ice

Fresh or fermented plums and syrup (see page 28)

Fresh or fermented cherries (see page 28)

Seltzer

Tarragon sprig or lemon verbena, for garnish

BOTTLING GAZOZ

Bottling gazoz is a fun, relatively simple, and refreshingly low-tech way to have a cool, colorful drink handy at a moment's notice. A home bottling apparatus, often referred to as a manual lever capper and more often associated with beer bottling, as well as the necessary bottles and caps, can easily be found online (see Shopping Guide, page 203). With this simple equipment, you can make sodas that will stay carbonated for weeks. I tend to shy away from putting fermented fruit in the bottle, since it's very hard to remove, so keep the process streamlined and simple.

Use a funnel to pour 2 tablespoons fruit syrup of your choice into a standard 12-ounce (355 ml) bottle (clear bottles are ideal, so you can see their beautiful contents).

Add an herb sprig, if you like (thyme and rosemary work well). You could also add a dried red chile or an aromatic leaf, like a bay leaf. Fill with seltzer or a combination of seltzer and jun (page 65), kefir (page 68), or kombucha (page 62).

Seal with a cap and refrigerate; it will keep for 2 to 3 weeks.

STONE
FRUIT
GAZOZ

Green Plum

Ice

Fermented green plums
and syrup (see page 28)

Green or red grapes

Small slice lime

Star fruit

Elderflower or other
edible blossoms

Mint or lemon verbena sprig

Seltzer

Apricot

Ice

Fermented apricot and syrup (see page 28)

Fresh apricot

Fermented black lime and syrup (see page 28, and see Note)

Fermented cardamom pod and syrup (see page 33)

Geranium leaves

Za'atar (hyssop) or oregano sprig

Zuta (white savory) or another flowering herb

Seltzer

» **Note:** Black limes (also known as limoo omani) are a dried, fermented lime traditionally used in soups and stews. See the Shopping Guide on page 203 for buying information.

Loquat

Ice

Fermented loquat and syrup
(see page 28)

Fermented sour plums and syrup (see page 28, and see Note)

Fermented lime and syrup
(see page 28, and see Note, page 106)

Fermented juniper berry and syrup (see page 28), or dried juniper berry

Fresh Thai bird chili

Orchid

Thai basil (or regular basil) sprig

Seltzer

» **Note:** When young, small, and rock-hard, most plums are sour and ideal for sweet fermentation. Persian sour plums can be found in farmers' markets in late spring. If you don't have access to a plum tree or farmers' market selling sour plums, you could substitute whole umeboshi, pickled Japanese sour plums, which are available at Asian markets and online at edenfoods.com.

Cherry

Ice

Fresh cherries

Hibiscus flowers and syrup
(follow the recipe for Rose Petal Syrup on page 51, replacing the rose petals with 1 cup [45 g] of dried hibiscus flowers)

Lime wedges

Fermented black peppercorns and syrup (see page 33)

Fermented cloves and syrup (see page 33)

Cinnamon stick

Rosemary sprig

Jasmine flowers

Lavender

Seltzer

Green Almond

Arugula flowers

Fresh lemon verbena

Savory

Lavender

Dried licorice root stick

Ice

Seltzer

Fermented green
almonds and syrup
(see page 28, and see Note)

» **Note:** Green almonds are found in farmers' markets
in early spring. If you can't find them, swap in a few
blanched whole almonds.

Lychee

Ice

Fermented lychees and syrup
(see page 28) or longan fruit or
canned lychees and syrup
(see Note)

Fermented black peppercorns
and syrup
(see page 33)

Pansy flowers

Lavender

Wormwood
(artemisia or prairie sage; see Shopping Guide,
page 203)

Seltzer

» **Note:** Longan fruit is similar in texture and flavor to lychee. You can find fresh
longans at Asian produce markets in season; if they're not available to you, use
fermented lychees and their syrup, or canned lychees and the syrup from the can.

Persimmon

Ice

Fresh and fermented persimmons and syrup (see page 28)

Fresh star fruit slices

Lemon slices

Lime slices

Fresh turmeric leaves

Mint sprig

Sinai sage sprig (see Note)

Seltzer

» **Note:** Sinai sage is a local variety with a minty flavor. Swap for regular sage.

Mulberry

Ice

Fermented white and red mulberries and syrup
(see page 28)

Fresh apricot

Fermented dried long pepper (or other fermented dried pepper) and syrup (see page 33, and see Note)

Orchid and calendula flowers

Fennel fronds

Lemon leaves

Lemongrass stalk

Seltzer

» **Note:** Mildly spicy, long pepper is indigenous to Africa and is used there in many cooking preparations. See the Shopping Guide on page 203 for buying information.

Apple Cinnamon

Ice

Fermented Asian pear and syrup (see page 28)

Fresh red apple slices

Fermented jujubes and syrup
(follow the recipe for Fermented Medjool
Dates and Syrup on page 49, replacing the
dates with jujubes)

Fresh mangosteen

Ginger puree (see page 44)

Dried barberries

Geranium leaves

Cinnamon stick

Seltzer

Mixed Berry and Jun

Ice

Fermented mixed berries (raspberry, blueberry, currants, blackberry) and syrup (see page 28)

Cypress leaves

Jasmine flowers or other flowers

Sage blossom

Seltzer

Jun (page 65)

Surinam Cherry

Ice

Fresh and fermented Surinam cherries

(see page 28, and see Note)

Lemongrass stalk

Caper flowers or another herb blossom

Fresh pomegranate or citrus leaves

Seltzer

» **Note:** Known as pitanga, Surinam cherries are tart and juicy. If you can't find them, seek out sour cherries when in season, or frozen year-round.

CITRUS
GAZOZ

Mixed Citrus

Ice

Fermented orange wedges and syrup (see page 28)

Fresh orange wedges

Fresh citron or yuzu
(see Note)

Fresh or dried allspice leaves
(see Shopping Guide, page 203)

Fresh cardamom leaves
(or any leaves of your choice)

Dried rose petals

Seltzer

» **Note:** These zesty citrus fruits can often be found at farmers' markets and Asian markets during the winter, when citrus is in season. If you can't find them, use limes.

Bitter Orange

Ice

Fermented bitter orange (chushchash; see Notes) slices or regular orange slices and syrup (see page 28)

Fermented grapefruit wedges and syrup (see page 28)

Fermented whole fresh jujubes and syrup (see page 28, and see Notes)

Lavender and basil leaves

Hibiscus flowers and syrup (follow the recipe for Rose Petal Syrup on page 51, replacing the rose petals with 1 cup [45 g] of dried hibiscus flowers)

Fresh hibiscus flower

Mint sprig

Seltzer

» **Notes:** Bitter oranges, also known as *chushchash*, are an early-winter crop in Israel and are free when picked from the communal trees that dot Tel Aviv. I pluck them and preserve them. You can do the same with Seville oranges, which can be found at farmers' markets during winter months. If you can't find Seville oranges, use any oranges you can find. Some Latin markets also sell bottled *jugo de naranja agria* ("sour orange juice"; see Shopping Guide, page 203). You can also use fermented regular oranges in place of the chushchash, then add a splash of Angostura bitters (see Shopping Guide, page 203).

Jujubes are also known as Chinese red date, and have a short growing season, so you're unlikely to find them fresh. Dried jujubes can be found at Chinese markets, and can be fermented by the same method used for Medjool dates (see page 49).

Triple Lime

Lemongrass stalk

Red endive spear

Zuta (white savory)

Fermented lime wheels and syrup (see page 28)

Fresh lime

Fresh finger lime
(see Shopping Guide, page 203)

Fresh or dried red currants

Seltzer

Orange

Ice

Fermented orange wedges and syrup (see page 28)

Sliced fresh orange

Chushchash (bitter orange) slice

Fresh kumquat

Mustard flowers

Mint sprig

Fresh, dried, or frozen curry leaves (see Shopping Guide, page 203)

Seltzer

OTHER
FRUIT
GAZOZ

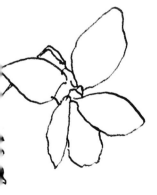

Pear

Ice

Fermented pears and pear syrup (see page 28)

Nigella (or black sesame) syrup
(see page 54)

Lime wedges

Myrtle flowers

Rehydrated chia seeds
(see Note)

White rose petals

Asparagus stalk

Seltzer

» **Note:** For one gazoz, cover 1 teaspoon chia seeds with
2 tablespoons cold water; rehydrate for 5 minutes, drain
and discard the water, and add the seeds to the glass.

Papaya Pineapple

Ice

Fermented diced papaya and syrup (see page 28)

Fermented diced pineapple and syrup (see page 28)

Rehydrated chia seeds
(see Note, page 143)

Fermented star anise pod and syrup (see page 33)

Ginger puree
(see page 44)

Fresh or dried allspice leaves
(see Shopping Guide, page 203)

Ox tongue leaves
(see Note)

Seltzer

» **Note:** A succulent plant with a neutral flavor, ox tongue (gasteria) can be found at nurseries and some plant shops. If you can't find it, swap in another leaf of your choice.

Pomegranate Kombucha

Ice

Fermented pomegranate
seeds and syrup (see page 28)

Fermented pomelo wedges
and syrup (see page 28)

Fermented black lime
(see page 28, and see Note, page 106)

Fresh lime wheel

Fermented cherry pits
(see page 28, and see Note)

Cinnamon stick

Lemon leaves

Seltzer

Kombucha (page 62)

» **Note:** In Moroccan cuisine, pits from the St. Lucie cherry are traditionally ground to make a spice known as *mahleb*, which is added to stews and desserts. Ferment cherry pits whole for a bittersweet addition to gazoz. (Though they are edible, use them in moderation—like apricot pits, cherry pits contain trace amounts of cyanide.)

Watermelon

Fresh lemon peel

Shiso leaves

Edible flowers

Seltzer

Ice

Fresh yellow and pink watermelon

Yellow watermelon syrup
(see page 46)

Fermented sycamore fig and syrup (see page 28, and see Note)

Rehydrated chia seeds
(see Note, page 143)

» **Note:** Sycamore figs, a variety mentioned in the Old Testament, grow freely on trees all over Tel Aviv in late spring. Most people have no idea that the small, delicious, fragrant fruit is edible, so I take advantage of its under-the-radar status, picking and preserving them every year. Add a slice of regular fig as a replacement.

Dragon Fruit

Ice

Fermented dragon fruit or kiwifruit and syrup (see page 28)

Fermented pear slice and syrup (see page 28)

Elderflower syrup, homemade (follow the recipe for Citrus Flower Syrup on page 47, replacing the citrus blossoms with fresh elderflowers, leaves and stems removed and discarded) or store-bought (see Shopping Guide, page 203)

Thai basil leaves or other basil leaves

Fresh or dried turmeric leaves

Mint sprig

Fenugreek leaves

Seltzer

Muscat Grape

Ice

Fermented muscat grapes
(or other grapes) and syrup
(see page 28)

Fresh kumquats

Fresh or dried allspice leaves
(see Shopping Guide, page 203)

Mustard flowers or other
flowering herbs or greens

Seltzer

Cactus Pear

Ice

Fermented cactus
pear (sabra) and syrup
(see page 28, and see Notes)

Fermented unripe apricots
and syrup (see page 28, and
see Notes)

Fermented cardamom pod
and syrup (see page 33)

Lime wheel

Chamomile flowers

Lemongrass stalk

Citrus leaves

Rosemary sprigs

Seltzer

» **Notes:** Considered one of Israel's national fruits, cactus pear (also known as *sabra* or prickly pear) has a thorny exterior and mildly sweet, pulpy flesh. It's seasonal and can be hard to find, so feel free to swap in fermented kiwifruit and syrup.

At the beginning of apricot season, I specifically seek out unripe fruits to ferment. If you can find still-green apricots, great; if not, unripe, preferably rock-hard apricots work very well.

FLORAL
GAZOZ

Rose

Ice

Rose petal syrup
(page 51)

Fresh food-grade
white rose petals

Pansy flower

Widow's tears flower,
or any edible flower

Lemon wedges

Lime wedges

Fresh grape leaves

Seltzer

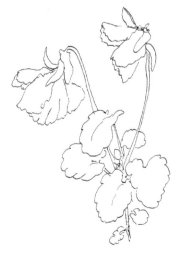

Hibiscus

Baby beet greens

Mint sprig

Seltzer

Ice

Hibiscus flowers and syrup (follow the recipe for Rose Petal Syrup on page 51, replacing the rose petals with 1 cup [45 g] of dried hibiscus flowers)

Citrus Flowers

Ice

Assorted citrus flowers

Unripe clementine slices

Fermented coriander seeds and syrup (see page 33)

Plum leaves

Savory (see Note)

Seltzer

» **Note:** Savory is a fragrant herb in the same family as oregano and marjoram. If you can't find savory, replace it with one of those.

Jasmine

Ice

Fermented jasmine flowers and syrup (see page 46)

Fermented sour plums and syrup (see page 28, and see Note, page 109)

Fresh jasmine flowers

Cinnamon leaves or other leaves

Seltzer

VEGETABLE GAZOZ

Carrot

Rosemary and thyme sprigs

Flowering basil sprig

Fermented dried hot chiles and syrup
(see page 33)

Multicolored carrot ribbons

Seltzer

Ice

Carrot syrup
(see page 43)

Turmeric puree
(see page 44)

Beet

Ice

Fermented beets and syrup
(see page 28) or fresh thinly sliced
beets and Beet Syrup (page 43)

Fresh pineapple guava
(see Note)

Papaya blossom

Blood of the Maccabees
(*Helichrysum sanguineum*), or other
edible flower

Lemon verbena sprig

Seltzer

» **Note:** Known as *fejoya* in Hebrew, pineapple guavas have a short season and are named for their distinctly floral, tropical aroma and flavor.

Tomato

Ice

Fermented black peppercorns and syrup
(see page 33)

Tomato Syrup
(page 43)

Fresh green tomato slices

Fresh cherry tomatoes
(with vines attached, if possible; see Note)

Kale, sage, and horseradish leaves

Seltzer

» **Note:** Tomato vines have a fragrance unique to them alone: fresh, grassy, and clean. If you can find clusters of cherry tomatoes on the vine, grab them and use them here!

Cucumber

Ice

Cucumber Syrup
(page 41)

Fresh cucumber ribbons

Fresh pear slice

Field peas and flowers

Mint sprig

Thai basil

Basil flower

Seltzer

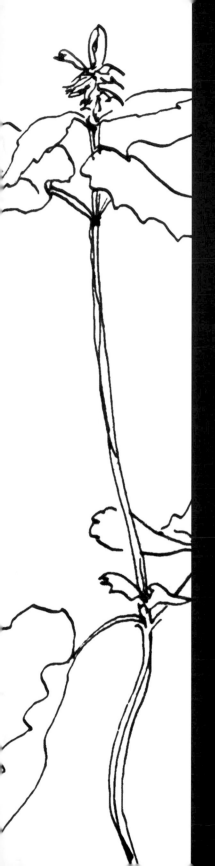

MILKSHAKE
GAZOZ

Peanut Butter

Ice

Peanut butter syrup
(see page 54)

Fermented coriander
seeds and syrup
(see page 33)

Fermented black
peppercorns and syrup
(see page 33)

Fresh plum slices

Purslane

Lemongrass stalk

Fresh fig wedges

Seltzer

Halvah

Lavender and
mint sprigs

Za'atar (hyssop) or
oregano sprig

Seltzer

Ice

Fermented sour plums
and syrup see page 28, and
see Note, page 109

Fresh yellow or red
cherries

Fresh strawberries

Halvah syrup (see page 54)

GAZOZ

Pistachio

Ice

Pistachio syrup
(see page 54)

Fermented raspberries
and syrup (see page 28)

Red currants

Cherries

Mint leaves

Fennel sprig

Arugula blossom or
any edible blossom

Seltzer

FANCIFUL
GAZOZ

Fig and Kefir

Sage and thyme sprigs

Asparagus flowers or
pea shoots

Calendula flowers

Fresh and fermented figs
and syrup (see page 28)

Fermented juniper berries
and syrup (see page 28)

Ice

Seltzer

Kefir (page 68)

Medjool Date

Ice

Fermented Medjool Dates and Syrup (page 49)

Fermented papaya and syrup (see page 28)

Fermented star anise pod and syrup (see page 33)

Dried licorice root stick (see Shopping Guide, page 203)

Fresh mango leaves (see Shopping Guide, page 203)

Calendula flower or other edible flower of your choice

Fenugreek leaves

Lemon verbena sprig

Seltzer

Pink Guava

Ice

Fermented guava and syrup
(see page 28)

Fermented whole pecans
(see Note)

Fermented cardamom pods
and syrup (see page 33)

Fresh or dried curry leaves
(see Shopping Guide, page 203)

Tarragon sprigs

Seltzer

» **Note:** I pick pecans, still in their shells, from trees in
the Tel Aviv area, and ferment them using the method
on page 28. You can substitute 2 or 3 shelled pecan
halves, either straight from the bag or fermented.

Sugar Apple

Ice

Rehydrated basil seeds
(see Notes)

Chopped fermented
sweetsop (sugar apple; see Notes)
and syrup (see page 28)

Hibiscus flowers and syrup
(follow the recipe for Rose Petal Syrup on
page 51, replacing the rose petals with 1 cup
[45 g] of dried hibiscus flowers)

Lemongrass stalk

Chrysanthemum

Arugula

Seltzer

» **Notes:** For one gazoz, cover 1 teaspoon basil seeds with 2 tablespoons cold water;
rehydrate for 5 minutes, drain and discard the water, and add the seeds to the glass.

Sugar apple, also known as sweetsop or custard apple, is a tropical fruit with large,
smooth seeds and a texture similar to lychee. It can be found at farmers' markets,
Asian markets, and tropical fruit stands or markets. If you can't find it fresh, look for
canned versions, or substitute fresh or canned lychees (and their syrup).

SHOPPING GUIDE

Beverage Components

ANGOSTURA BITTERS
Made from orange peels and
botanicals, these bitters—
available at liquor stores and
supermarkets—stand in well
for *chushchash* (bitter orange;
see page 132).

BITTER ORANGE JUICE
Use bitter orange juice to
replace *chushchash* (bitter
orange; see page 132). Look
for it under its Spanish name,
jugo de naranja agria, in Latin
markets and mainstream
supermarkets.

ELDERFLOWER SYRUP
Elderflower syrup by D'arbo
can be found at liquor stores,
specialty stores, and online.

FERMENTATION INGREDIENTS
For jun, fermentaholics.com
sells a reliable organic live
starter kit, which contains a
SCOBY and starter tea. For
kombucha, kombuchacompany
.com has a neatly packaged
SCOBY and starter tea.

Kombucha.com sells a good
tea blend for making both
jun and kombucha. To make
the water kefir on page 68,
seek out water kefir grains at
culturesforhealth.com.

FINGER LIMES
Finger limes can be
ordered online in season
from Melissa's produce
(melissasproduce.com) and
found at farmers' markets.

GINGER AND
TURMERIC SHOTS
Ginger and turmeric shots
can be found at juice shops
like Jamba Juice and Juice
Generation, and at markets like
Erewhon and Whole Foods.

HERBS AND SPICES
Fresh, dried, and frozen curry
leaves can often be found in
Indian and Asian markets,
or can be ordered from
kalustyans.com or ishopindian
.com. Dried allspice leaves can
be found at kalustyans.com,

along with dried licorice root sticks. Look for basil seeds in Asian markets.

HIBISCUS FLOWERS AND ORANGE OIL
Purchase from kalustyans.com.

LONG PEPPER
Look for these in African markets and Asian markets and at kalustyans.com.

NUT BUTTERS AND TAHINI
Many of the recipes on pages 183–189 call for pure nut butters. It's important to buy nut butters with no added oils, sweeteners, or preservatives. For pistachio, try the Pistachio Factory; for tahini, try Soom, Seed + Mill, Al Arz, or Har Bracha. For hazelnut, try Vör; and for peanut, try Barney Butter Bare Smooth.

BLACK LIME (LIMOO OMANI)
Look for them at Persian and Middle Eastern stores or online at kalustyans.com.

Equipment

BAR SPOON
cocktailkingdom.com

FERMENTATION JAR COVERS
kombuchacamp.com

FINE-MESH STRAINERS
Boroughkitchen.com sells smaller fine-mesh strainers, or try zabars.com. OXO makes an 8-inch (20 cm) version that is useful when making kombucha, jun, and kefir.

GLASS JARS AND BOTTLES
bascousa.com

HOME BOTTLING MACHINE
To make bottled gazoz like the ones on pages 100–101, search online for "manual beer capping machine" or "bottle cap sealer" or "bottle capper." You can buy bottles, caps, and labels, too.

STRAW SPOONS
uncommongoods.com

SUSTAINABLE STRAWS
Glass and metal straws are available at simplystraws.com. Bamboo straws are available at junglestraws.com and bambuhome.com.

READING
RESOURCES

Though this particular reading list could be filled with dozens of titles, here are a few good books to help you further understand fermentation, as well as how to identify edible plants, herbs, and flowers.

The Art of Fermentation by Sandor Ellix Katz

The Edible Flower Garden by Kathy Brown

Field Guide to Edible Wild Plants by Bradford Angier

The Noma Guide to Fermentation by René Redzepi and David Zilber

Wild Fermentation by Sandor Ellix Katz

ACKNOWLEDGMENTS

To Lia and David, your short visit to my shop led to a life-changing proposal, which made a dream come true—a dream I didn't even know I had. Much magic has been made since that moment, and for that, a huge thank-you.

To Judy Pray and the team at Artisan Books, thank you so much for your professionalism, for your patience and wisdom, and for guiding me along this incredible ride—my deepest gratitude.

To the amazing Adeena Sussman, who agreed without a moment's hesitation to come along for this journey, something I don't for one minute take for granted. You made everything so easy, relaxed, and beautiful, and it wouldn't have been possible without your experience, talent, willingness, and love for this book. Many, many thanks!

To Dan Perez, for your talent, your determination, and conjuring your special brand of sorcery whenever it was needed. For your calmness and vision, for always being there for us, and of course, for your handiwork—these stunning photos.

To Moshe Prizmant, my partner at Café Levinsky, for your support, for seeing the long game, for tolerating my occasional insanity, for the tough times we've endured together along the way, and for our wonderful organic farm that wouldn't have been possible without you.

To my amazing partner, Yifat Touva, for your support and for all your moments of inspiration, which led to so, so many beautiful things! My thanks and love.

To my fantastic staff at Café Levinsky, for your hard work every day, for sharing my love of fermentation, for your curiosity, and for the million smiles we've smiled together in this special endeavor.

To the talented Neta Lou, for your generosity of spirit and the beautiful gazoz you created, and for all the days you devoted to the photo shoots along the way to this incredible book.

And of course, a million thanks to the universe, for all the stars in the sky that watch over us.

INDEX

ABOUT THE AUTHORS

Benny Briga is the chef/owner of Café Levinsky 41, located in Tel Aviv's trendy Levinsky Market. He lives in Tel Aviv, Israel, and you can find him on Instagram at @cafe_levinsky41.

Adeena Sussman is the author of *Sababa*, and co-writer of the bestsellers *Cravings* and *Hungry for More* by Chrissy Teigen. She also lives in Tel Aviv, Israel. Follow her on Instagram at @adeenasussman.